GORILLAS OF THE IMPENETRABLE FOREST:

THE MOUNTAIN GORILLAS OF BWINDI

BY CAROL SCHALLER CARMICHAEL

ISBN-13: 978-1544963426
ISBN-10: 1544963424

For Susie N, who is not a complainer
For Annie O, the Brave Enabler
For the mysterious Claire C
For Marilyn S - this is not the last trip
For Garth who introduced me to his favorite gorilla family
And always and forever, for Doug

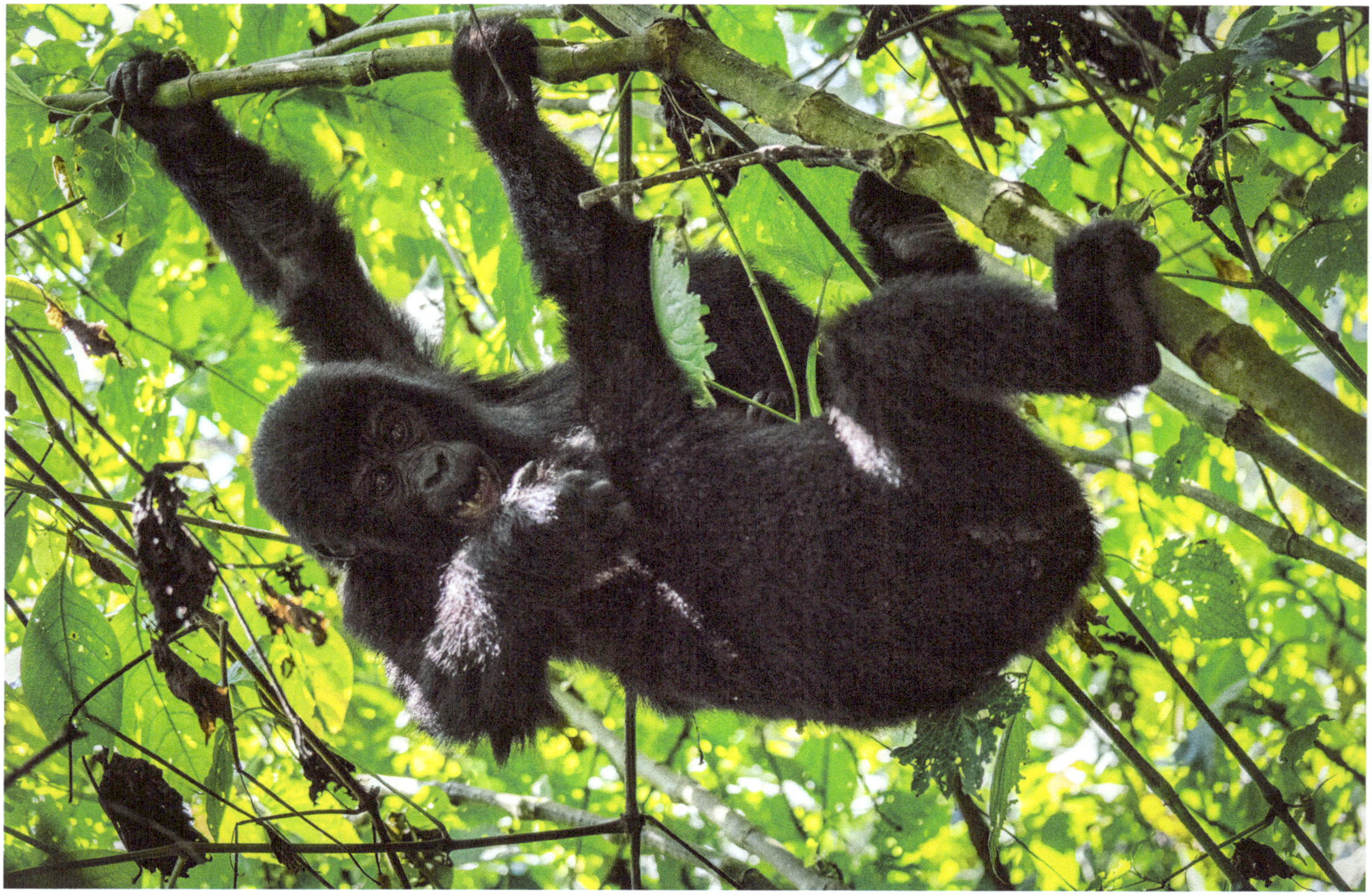

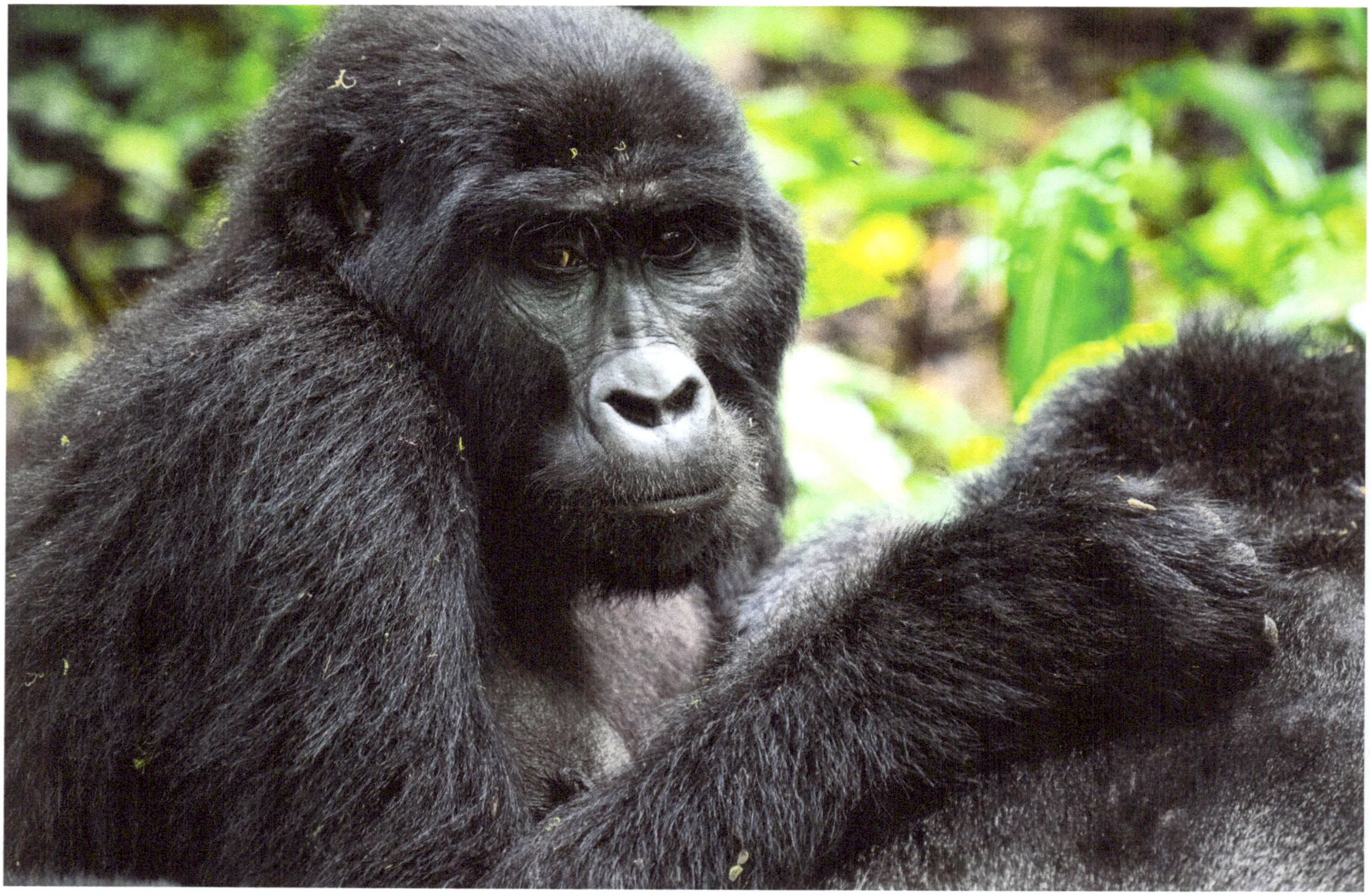